Staying Happy

by Patricia J. Murphy

Series consultants: Sonja Green, MD, and
Distinguished Professor Emerita Ann Nolte, PhD,
Department of Health Sciences, Illinois State University

Pull Ahead Books

Lerner Publications Company • Minneapolis

To my happy, little family—with love, PJM

The author would like to thank Dan Baker, PhD; Edward M. Hallowell, MD; Robert Schwebel, PhD; and Catherine "Kitty" Creswell for their assistance—as well as all the happy people she encountered while writing this book. Choose happiness!

The publisher thanks Sonja Green, MD, and Ann Nolte, distinguished professor emerita of the Dept. of Health Sciences at Illinois State University, for their assistance with this book.

Lerner Publications Company
A division of Lerner Publishing Group
241 First Avenue North
Minneapolis, MN 55401 U.S.A.

Website address: www.lernerbooks.com

Words in **bold type** are explained in a glossary on page 31.

Library of Congress Cataloging-in-Publication Data

Murphy, Patricia J., 1963–
    Staying happy / by Patricia J. Murphy.
        p.   cm.
    Includes index.
    ISBN-13: 978-0-8225-2796-1 (lib. bdg. : alk. paper)
    ISBN-10: 0-8225-2796-0 (lib. bdg. : alk. paper)
    1. Happiness—Juvenile literature. I. Title.
BF575.H27.M87 2006
152.4'2–dc22   2004028890

Manufactured in the United States of America
1 2 3 4 5 6 – JR – 11 10 09 08 07 06

Joanne smiles. Her eyes are bright.
She sings and dances around. She
feels happy.

Happiness makes people feel **peaceful** and well. Feeling happy adds to people's lives.

What makes
you happy?

No one feels happy all the time.
Sometimes people feel sad, lonely, or
afraid. Sometimes people worry.

Sometimes people feel **stress**.
How does stress make you feel?

Stress may make you feel **anxious** or under **pressure**. It may make your stomach or head hurt. It may keep you awake at night.

But some stress is okay. It helps you do your best in school or learn a new skill.

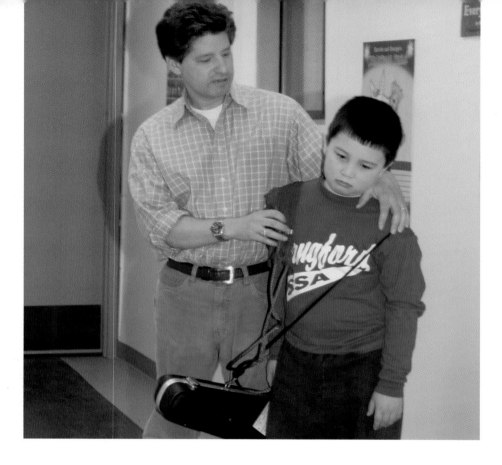

Vincent is busy with school, chores, soccer, violin, and Cub Scouts. He never has time to **relax**. Vincent feels stress.

Vincent talks to his dad. Vincent wants
more time for himself. He decides to
take a break from soccer.

Vincent draws pictures instead.
Drawing gives him quiet time.
What do you do when you feel stress?

Talking to someone can help. It lets you find out what is causing you to feel stress. Then you can figure out a way to feel better.

Beth has trouble with reading.
Her friends at school seem
to be better at reading.

Beth feels stress when she reads in class. Her heart beats fast, and her hands sweat. She feels like she is going to cry.

Beth talks to her mom. Beth asks her teacher for extra help with reading.

Beth **practices** at home. She begins to feel better. What do you do when you have trouble with schoolwork?

Lily's friend Rose is having a party.
Rose didn't invite Lily. Lily feels lonely.
She is afraid she has no friends.

Lily talks to her grandma. Lily decides
to throw her own party. She invites her
grandma and her doll Bailey.

Lily did something to make herself
feel better.

What do you do when you feel
lonely or afraid?

We all have times when we feel worried, sad, or lonely. But there are things we can do to feel happy again.

We can share our feelings with someone we trust. We can think about what might help us feel better.

Do things that you love to do. Laugh
and have fun!

But don't try to do too much. Doing
too much can cause more stress.

Try to eat right and **exercise**.
You should also get plenty of rest.
Being **healthy** makes you happy.

Feeling happy adds to your life. And
you can help yourself feel happy!

Learn to Relax

Learning to relax can help your body deal with stress.
Find a quiet place and try one of these:

■ Practice deep breathing. Take a deep breath. Pull
your stomach in as you breathe in. Then blow the air
out slowly and let your stomach out as you blow out.
Repeat. Deep breathing helps your body to relax.

■ Close your eyes and picture a peaceful place. Where
are you? What are you doing? How are you feeling?
Open your eyes when you feel relaxed.

■ Exercise every day. Moving around helps your body
deal with stress.

■ Grab a nap. Take a 15-minute "catnap" when you
need one. It will help give you energy.

■ Let your muscles rest. Lie down. Let your face get
tight, then relax. Make each part of your body tight,
like making a fist. Then let go and relax. Try this one
part at a time. Start with your head, neck, shoulders,
arms, middle, and legs. End at your toes.

Top Five Ways to Share Your Feelings

It's healthy to share your feelings.

1. Talk to someone you trust.

2. Make a feelings journal.

3. Write a poem.

4. Paint a picture.

5. Do a dance.

Books and Websites

Books

Anholt, Catherine. *What Makes Me Happy?* Cambridge, MA: Candlewick Press, 1995.

Ayer, Eleanor H. *Everything You Need to Know about Stress.* New York: Rosen Publishing Group, 2001.

Evans, Lezlie. *Sometimes I Feel Like a Storm Cloud.* New York: Mondo, 1998.

Vail, Rachel. *Sometimes I'm Bombaloo.* New York: Scholastic Press, 2002.

Websites

Bam! Body and Mind: Centers for Disease Control and Prevention
http://www.bam.gov

Kidshealth
http://www.kidshealth.org/kid/feeling/

Glossary

anxious: to feel worried or nervous about something

exercise: movement you do to keep healthy

healthy: being fit or well or something that makes you fit or well

peaceful: calm, quiet, relaxed

practices: does something over and over again to get better at it

pressure: a feeling of being pushed to do something

relax: to let go or be calm

stress: a feeling of strain or pressure

Index

Photo Acknowledgments

The photographs in this book appear courtesy of: Digital Vision Royalty Free, cover, p. 4; © age fotostock/SuperStock, pp. 3, 8, 22, 23, 29; Comstock Images, p. 5; © Marilyn Conway/SuperStock, p. 6; © Todd Strand/Independent Picture Service, pp. 7, 10–17, 19, 20, 25; © Charles Gupton/CORBIS, p. 9; © Beth Johnson/Independent Picture Service, p. 18; © Richard Heinzen/SuperStock, p. 21; © Royalty-Free/Corbis, p. 24; © BananaStock/SuperStock, p. 26; EyeWire by Getty Images, p. 27.

My First...
School Day

First published in the UK in 2009 by
QED Publishing
A Quarto Group Company
226 City Road
London EC1V 2TT
www.qed-publishing.co.uk

A catalogue record for this book is available
from the British Library.

ISBN 978 1 84835 164 6

Author Eve Marleau
Illustrator Michael Garton
Consultants Shirley Bickler and Tracey Dils
Designer Elaine Wilkinson

Publisher Steve Evans
Creative Director Zeta Davies
Managing Editor Amanda Askew

Printed and bound in China

The words in **bold** are
explained in the glossary
on page 24.

My First...
School Day

Eve Marleau and Michael Garton

QED Publishing

On Monday, Dad takes Kai to **primary school**. It's Kai's first day and he's a bit worried.

"Dad, I don't want to go to school. I won't know anyone and I will miss Barney."

"I'm sure you'll make some new friends. All the other boys and girls will be feeling exactly the same as you," says Dad.

"Hello! Welcome to
Reception Class.
My name is Miss James."

"Hello," says Dad. "This is Kai."

"Hello, Kai. Would you like
to sit with Lucas and Max?"
Kai nods.

"Good morning, Reception Class. Please sit on the carpet so I can take the **register**."

"When I call out your name, say 'Yes, Miss James' and tell us all something about yourself."

"Ama?"

Yes, Miss James. My dad is a firefighter.

"First, I'm going to put you in special **groups**.
You will work in these groups every day.

"Ben, Lisa, Jane,
Steven and Alison are
the yellow rockets."

"Ama, Clare, Lucas,
Toby and Susie are
the green rockets."

"Max, Julia, Caroline, Tamzin and Nieve are the blue rockets."

"Kai, Sarah, Daniel, Matthew and Fran are the red rockets."

11

"This morning, you're going to draw your favourite thing. Then I'll put all your drawings on the wall."

Kai draws Barney, Sarah draws a pony and Fran draws a teddy bear.

Max draws
a red car.

Lucas draws an **astronaut.**

Ring! Ring! It's break time.

The children each take an apple
from Miss James and go outside.

Julia, Caroline and Nieve sit on
the bench eating their apples.

Kai plays catch with Max and Matthew.

Clare, Lucas and Toby play tag.

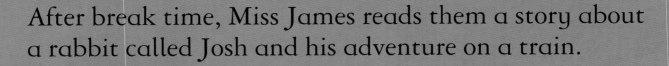

After break time, Miss James reads them a story about a rabbit called Josh and his adventure on a train.

"WOOOO WOOOOO!"

Miss James reads.

"Pull the train's whistle, children."

"Woooo WOOOOO!"

says the whole class as they move around
the room. Kai says it as loudly as he can.

After story time, Miss James asks the children about their favourite animals.

18

19

Ring! Ring!

The bell rings
at 12 o'clock.

20

"Normally it would be time for lunch.
Today, as it's your very first day,
you can go home now."

"Yay!"

21

Outside the school, Mum and Barney wait for Kai. "Did you have a nice morning?"

"Yes, I did!

I drew a picture of Barney."

Glossary

Astronaut A person who travels into space in a rocket or spacecraft.

Break time A short time between lessons.

Group Several people who have been put together.

Primary school A school for children aged between four and 11.

Reception Class The youngest class in primary school.

Register A list of the children's names in a class.